FOLKLORE AND
IN THE
MABINOGION

A LECTURE
DELIVERED AT THE NATIONAL MUSEUM OF WALES
ON 27 OCTOBER 1950

BY

W. J. GRUFFYDD

*Published jointly with
the National Museum of Wales*

British Library Cataloguing-in-Publication Data
A catalogue record for this book is available from
the British Library

FOLKLORE AND MYTH
IN THE MABINOGION

For the purpose of this lecture, ' folklore ' does not mean folk-culture in its various manifestations as you can see it exhibited and exemplified at St. Fagans and in the famous museums of Scandinavia, but the traditional beliefs and legends of the folk as distinct from the more respectable beliefs and legends which are accepted as facts, and which are called Theology and History respectively. The basis, however, of the greater part of folklore, in the sense in which I use it, is the theology and history of the past handed down from generation to generation and losing, in the passage of time, most of the indications of their original significance. Indeed the line between theology and history on the one hand and folklore beliefs and legends on the other may sometimes be very thin. For example, the existence of a personal Devil is a respectable and orthodox theological tenet, but that has not prevented his very unorthodox entrance into the folklore of the modern nations. Did he not, for instance, build the famous bridge over the river Mynach in Cardiganshire ? And King Alfred may very well have burnt the good wife's cakes ; if he did, then that story is sober history, but sober history or not, it has now become a folk-legend in England.

You will notice that the title contains the two words, ' Folklore ' and ' Myth.' I have used both words because I do not wish at the outset to prejudge the issue whether almost all folklore is ultimately derived from myth, that is, from a primitive belief about the gods, or is of a more lowly origin and to be explained in terms of mass psychology or, as I think more likely, from a mixture of both.   Further I must explain that I use the term ' primitive ' comparatively. That is to say, ' primitive beliefs,' as far as this lecture is concerned, are only primitive because they belong to a kind of culture which existed before our era, and not necessarily because they are derived from a rude, undeveloped, and inferior state of society.   Our knowledge of social conditions in Britain before the Roman Conquest is necessarily limited in spite of the magnificent work done by archaeologists among whom the staff of this museum has a very distinguished place.   In short, when I use the term ' primitive,' I have in mind priority in time and custom and not an assessment of human values.

A further point.   I have confined myself to one section only of folklore as I have defined it, namely the legends and beliefs about the *Tylwyth Teg*, the Welsh Fairies.   There are other folklore details in the Mabinogion on which I cannot touch in this lecture, such as the onomastic stories (stories designed to explain a name) ;   survivals of primitive society as seen in the avoidance of such terms as ' marriage,' ' husband,' and the abnegation of Christian baptism ;   old games such as the ' Badger in the Bag ' ;   beliefs about *dihenydd*, ' fate ' ;   the swearing of a *tynged*, ' destiny ' upon a person, and even one survival of belief which might be related to the development of the *Tylwyth Teg*, namely the existence of an old race of giants as in *Branwen* and in the legends of Ireland.   I hope to be able to deal with all these matters elsewhere.

2

If you consult any standard book on Welsh folklore such as Wirt Sikes's *British Goblins* or Sir John Rhŷs's *Celtic Folklore* or Professor Gwynn Jones's *Welsh Folklore* or Hugh Evans's *Tylwyth Teg*, you will find that the place of honour is occupied by stories about the Welsh variety of Fairies who are called in Welsh *Y Tylwyth Teg*, ' the Fair People.'   And rightly, because with the exception of a few ghost stories which follow a well-defined formula, and some traditional beliefs and customs mostly connected with death, the bulk of Welsh folklore is concerned with *Y Tylwyth Teg*. Further, the fairy stories of Wales have a character of their own which distinguishes them from those of the rest of Britain and even to a certain extent from the more or less cognate tales of Ireland and Gaelic Scotland.

Now the name *Tylwyth Teg* is curious, so curious indeed that it is surprising that no one, to my knowledge, has questioned its authenticity,—that is, whether it is an old Welsh name to designate the other-world people of folklore, like the Irish *sídhe* which is found in the earliest literature, or whether it is of comparatively late origin. That the name *Tylwyth Teg* cannot be the original designation of the other-world beings known in England as ' fairies ' can easily be seen on consideration of its etymological history. It does not occur in our older literature and there is no suggestion of it in the Mabinogion and the other Romances associated with them in the manuscripts. In short, tales of the *Tylwyth Teg*, under that specific name, belong to the comparatively modern folklore of Wales, though, as I hope to prove in this lecture, the material from which they were formed is ancient and abundantly exemplified in the Mabinogion. It should be noted that the name *Tylwyth Teg* is not the designation of the Fairies in every part of Wales ; in South Wales the usual name is *Bendith y Mamau*, ' The Blessing of the Mothers.' Rhŷs and others have suggested that the *Mamau* represent the old Celtic *Matronae* and *Matres* of whose universal worship we have abundant archaeological and historical evidence. The Mother of the Immemorial Prisoner in *Culhwch* is Modron, which represents exactly the old Celtic *mātrŏna* whose altars still survive. As to *Bendith* ' blessing,' I can only suggest that it is used to propitiate the fairies just as the Greeks spoke of the Furies as *Eumenides*, ' the Gracious Ones.' If this is correct then *Bendith y Mamau* is a propitiatory term for

Melltith y Mamau, ' The Curse of the Matres.'

Let us now consider the name *Tylwyth Teg.* I have been unable to find any instance of it before that which occurs in *Cywydd y Niwl,* attributed to Dafydd ap Gwilym. Here the poet describes himself as lost in the mist which he calls

Hir barthlwyth y Tylwyth Teg

—' A vast accumulation on the forecourt of the *Tylwyth Teg*'. He has lost his way on the moorland, and the description is therefore particularly apt since the *Tylwyth Teg* are traditionally associated with the troubles of forlorn and benighted travellers. The *cywydd,* as I have said, belongs to the Dafydd ap Gwilym period, or at least to the first quarter of the fifteenth century. Why then, it may be asked, is Welsh literature before 1400 both prose and verse, silent about the *Tylwyth Teg* ? It is because *their name shows that they were not, so to speak, constituted as a people until after the development of the Arthurian tales of France and their later introduction into the literature of England ;* until, in fact a cycle of romance had been created which was based on ' the matter of Britain ' and which was necessarily later than the original legendary material of Wales which is incorporated in the Mabinogion.

The name *Tylwyth Teg* betrays its late origin. The first part *tylwyth* roughly corresponds to the English ' household ' or ' family ' and *teg* means ' fair ' ; the whole phrase can be translated ' The Fair Folk ' or, possibly, ' The Fair Household.' Now it is obvious that *teg* is to be explained in one of three ways. Either (1) it is a translation of the English *fairy,* or (2) the English *fairy* is a translation of the Welsh *teg,* or (3) the name was given independently in Welsh and English to designate the ' fair ' people. Fortunately, we need not hesitate between the three explanations, because the derivation of English *fairy* shows that the Welsh *teg* must be a mistranslation of it, due to a complete misunderstanding of its meaning. *Fairy* has nothing whatever to do with *fair,* ' beautiful ' or ' blonde,' which is from the Old English *faeger.* The first known instance of *fairy* in English is in the form *feiri* and is dated 1310. *Feiri* is derived from Old French *faerie*, (Mod. French *féerie*) which is the collective form of *fée*, (Mod. French *fée*). *Fae* is from the Latin *fata*, ' the Fates ' ; the same word is found in the Italian *fata Morgana* ' the fée Morgain,' the name of a mirage. It will be seen therefore that *fairy* has no connection with *fair*, ' teg '; the similarity is purely accidental. The fact that Welsh *teg* shows a misapprehension of the meaning of ' fairy ' due to the accident of similarity proves that the English name is the original, and that the Welsh is modelled upon it. There are of course plenty of instances in every language of this kind of mistranslation ; I need only remind you of that well-worn cliché ' psychological moment ' which is due to a confusion between the neuter word *moment* ' momentum ' in the original German phrase and the masculine *moment* ' moment of time.' So that the word *teg* in *Tylwyth Teg*, being due to a misunderstanding of the English, shows that its use in this particular context is late and derivative.

But that does not mean that the history, so to speak, of the *Tylwyth Teg* is either late or derivative. It means that this other-world people of Wales appears in a new dress cut according to the fashion in vogue in England. It means that the original legends and beliefs concerning the other-world folk have been grouped together in the popular mind to form the history of one unified people under a new name. Or I should rather say, perhaps, that whereas they were before nameless, they have now become identified with the English Fairy Folk. We shall see that this identification has obscured the high lineage of the *Tylwyth Teg*.

3

The stories current in Wales about the *Tylwyth Teg* fall into three well-defined classes which owe their origin to three different sources; in other words the *Tylwyth Teg*

like many more politically important nations is composed
of at least three different ' racial ' elements.   The first two
may be regarded as forming together the main body of the
Tylwyth Teg, and the third element is perhaps an alien
immigration in later times.   The first element is derived
from mythology, whether at one remove or more it is
unnecessary here to decide ;   the second element is derived
from history, not indeed recorded history, but the imagina-
tively distorted recollection of the folk.   Shelley speaks of
Time as ' like a many-coloured dome of glass staining the
white radiance of eternity ';   his great phrase may be justly
applied to humbler things.   Time also stains with its own
colours the white radiance of historical facts.

The three elements are :

1.   The Welsh *Annwfn* (the Other-world of gods and
heroes).   I cannot give here a precise definition of what
Annwfn meant to our ancestors.   Sometimes it is regarded
as the Land of the Dead, something like the Greek Hades,
presided over by the ' dark ' divinities ;   sometimes it is
the Land of Youth and Promise, *Tir na nÒg*, the home of
bliss and harmony ;   sometimes it is a mysterious border
country, menacing the land of the living, the actual
world.   As we shall see, a great part of the Four Branches
is concerned with the affairs of *Annwfn* and its lords.

2.   The second element is the folk recollection of an
aboriginal people living in inaccessible parts of the
countryside, having no contact with the dominant race,
and living in fear and suspicion of them.

3.   The third element which seems distinct from the
first two, may for the sake of convenience be called by a
name borrowed from our Cornish brothers,—the Pixies.
Whether these are part of the Welsh folk tradition or
have been introduced later through England from
Teutonic folklore I am unable to decide.   They comprise
the mischievous, puckish and irresponsible portion of the
fairy population of Wales.   Whatever their origin and

at whatever period they joined the men of *Annwfn* and the men of the moorland solitudes they are definitely authenticated in Welsh folklore.

I have placed these three classes in the order of their importance and in the probable order of their entry into folklore, but it will be convenient to deal first with the second and third classes.

4

One of the most widely-spread of all the fairy tales is that of the Lady of the Lake ; the typical form of this *märchen* is the Legend of Llyn y Fan Fach in Carmarthenshire which purports to explain how a famous mediaeval family of physicians living at Myddfai obtained their knowledge of healing from an ancestor who had, some time in the twelfth century, married a fée, the Lady of the Lake of Y Fan Fach. This type of legend is widely spread all over Wales, and though all the features are not contained in any one version, they may be gathered from a comparison of all the versions. It would take more time than I have at my disposal if I were to attempt to make a full recension of these various versions ; many of the details are what might be called local variations and derive their interest and importance, not from the original tradition of the Lady of the Lake, but from the light they throw on the social and cultural con- ditions of those who have handed it down to posterity. The following account, however, will be found to contain most of those features which are obviously essential to the story.

A young countryman happened to be one day near a lake in a wild and uninhabited part near his home. He saw a woman, the most beautiful that mortal eyes had ever beheld, sitting on a bank on the lake-side. He offered her the bread and cheese which he brought with him and tried to touch her, but she kept away from him, and taunted him with the quality of his bread :

> Cras dy fara,
> Nid hawdd fy nala.

' You with the baked bread, you will not easily catch me,' and then disappeared in the lake. Next day he came again, this time bringing unbaked bread, but with no better result. The lady still evaded him and said :

> Llaith dy fara,
> Ti ni fynna'.

' You with the moist bread, I will not have you.' His mother seeing that there was a spell connected with the bread, gave him some soft-baked bread (perhaps unleavened) for his third attempt. This time when he went to the lake he beheld a herd of beautiful cows, white with spots of red, walking along its surface, followed by the maiden. He offered her the soft-baked bread and she allowed him to approach her. After much coyness and argument she consented to marry him on condition that he would never touch her with iron. (In some versions, on condition that she did not receive from him *Tri ergyd diachos*, ' three blows without cause.' I regard this as an obvious contamination from a triadic tradition such as *Trydedd anfad palfawd*, ' the three evil slaps,' which is quoted in *Mabinogi Branwen*). The next time her father appeared with her, and told him that he would consent to their marriage on condition that he could pick her out from among her five sisters. The sisters were so similar that he was unable to point to the one he loved, but she helped him by putting forward her toe whereas the others kept their feet together. When she finally came to him she brought with her the herd of marvellous cows, sheep, and goats which she counted by fives. They lived happily and had many children. The cows gave three times as much milk as those of their neighbours. She objected, however, to have the green sward in front of the house ploughed. After they were married he did not see her people again except when they came to market, a small queer looking folk with sallow complexions, but they said never a word, and used to point at what they wanted. After many years she went one day to the paddock to catch a horse. She was so unskilful that her husband came to help her, but the horse was by this time frightened and in trying to stop him the husband threw the bridle with the iron attached. He missed the horse and the bit struck his wife. ' You have now struck me with iron ' she cried, and disappeared in the lake, calling her cattle to follow her.

Rhŷs, in his great work, *Celtic Folklore*, has listed the characteristics of the *Tylwyth Teg* as contained in the different versions. I quote his words (p. 660) :

' the sallowness of their skin and the smallness of their stature, their dwelling underground, their dislike of iron and the comparative poverty of their homes in the matter of useful articles of furniture, their deeprooted objection of the green sward being broken up by the plough, the success of the fairy wife in attending to the domestic animals and the dairy, the limited range generally of the fairies' ability to count ; and lastly one may perhaps mention their using a language of their own which would imply a time when the little people understood no other, and explain why they should be represented doing their marketing without uttering a syllable to anybody.'

Rhŷs's list may contain one misconception,—namely ' their dwelling underground.' This detail has crept in, I believe, from the first element in fairy lore which we shall consider later ; the essential feature of the type of legend which I have summarized above is that the Fairy Folk dwell in a lake. He has also omitted two important characteristics—the apparent similarity of the members of the Fairy Folk—that is why the countryman in the story was unable to distinguish the woman he wanted from her sisters,—and their unacquaintance with horses and their ways.

Rhŷs has, without going very deeply into archaeological details, declared his belief that these characteristics of the Welsh Fairy Folk have an ethnological significance. I make no apology for accepting his explanation which has also been put forward by other scholars. Some later researchers however, have cold-shouldered this theory, but I think that their attitude is due to ignoring the fact that the fairy folklore of Wales is of mixed origin, that incongruous elements are combined in its composition, and that primitive inhabitants of more than one period may have contributed to its totality. It often happens that when a cliché of scholarship becomes discredited, a perfectly sound explanation which has become fortuitously attached to it suffers the same fate. It happened in this case : romantic writers used to enlarge on the ' Iberian ' element in the Welsh nation,—Sir Owen Edwards in his *Wales* went so far as to publish a picture of the poet Islwyn as a typical ' Iberian,' and to suggest a fanciful contrast between the dreamy and artistic ' Iberian ' and the practical hard-headed Celt. All this has gone, and with it, quite illogically, the ethnological explanation of this particular type of fairy folklore. But to reject it is to throw out the baby with the bath-water.

It is probable that, when the iron-using Celtic invaders became the dominant race, the previous inhabitants, perhaps for a very long time, lived a separate and secluded life of their own in some kind of lake dwelling or in isolated and inaccessible parts. Their manner of life and their language were different from that of the newer Celtic settlers ; they may have had no ovens as the Celts had so that their bread was different ; perhaps it was unleavened. They were small and had a sallow skin ; it may be they had a ' Mongolian ' type of countenance, so that the Celts could not distinguish one from the other just as we today find it difficult to distinguish the Chinese. They were mostly a pastoral people and horses were unknown to them. They had a different system of counting from the Celts, (who

perhaps later, when the barriers between the two peoples
were removed, partly adopted their system in the numbers
from 15 to 19). Finally iron was something terrible,
because it was new and *was the specific symbol of the invading
race.* In short, this type of legend preserves a folk-recollection of the aboriginal inhabitants and their impact on the
Celtic settlers, and it is to be noted that, whereas in stories
belonging to the first and third elements in my classification,
the strange folk are called *Tylwyth Teg,* there are many
versions of the Lady of the Lake type where the name is
not mentioned, for instance in the long and detailed *versio
princeps* of the Legend of Llyn y Fan Fach given by Rees of
Tonn in the introduction to his *Physicians of Myddfai.* In
other words, the *Tylwyth Teg* have not yet completely
absorbed the strange folk of the Lake legends.

5

The third element is the Pixies, though of course that
name does not occur in Welsh. In all North-European
folklore there is a tradition of irresponsible and mischievous
beings, sometimes benevolent but rather oftener malevolent,
making stealthy raids on the well-ordered existence of
normal people. In Wales the extent of their activities is
somewhat restricted, compared for instance with that of the
pixies of Cornwall and the goblins of Teutonic countries
and the only really significant contribution which they
seem to have made to the lore of the *Tylwyth Teg* is, first,
their gifts of money and services in the dairy, (which
probably betrays contamination by the second element),
and secondly their mischief-making in displacing articles of
furniture and so on, and in changing the property of the
Welsh family by substituting their own, especially by taking
away new-born babies and leaving children of their own
in their place. How old this element is in Welsh folklore
it is difficult to tell ; it is possible that a belief in mischievous
imp-like spirits is natural to all communities living in the
country—Fairies in all lands wisely avoid the towns—but

the part that the Pixies play in Welsh folklore is comparatively small, and the stories about them have neither the romance of the Lake legends of the second element nor the nostalgic mystery of the fairy Elysium of the first.

6

Now what traces are to be found in the Mabinogion and Romances of the second and third elements of our classification ? It is outside my province to consider the French versions of original British themes, *Arglwyddes y Ffynnawn*, *Geraint*, *Peredur* and those over which the magic of Merlin, that high priest of *féerie*, holds sway, but in the rest of the collection (The Four Branches, *Culhwch*, *Macsen*, *Lludd a Llefelys* and *Rhonabwy*) it is possible to discern traces of the folklore attached to the Lake legends and to the Pixies. One striking feature common to the Mabinogion and the Fairy stories is the coyness of the fairy women and their half-reluctant ' leading on ' of the men who have fallen in love with them. Pwyll fails to catch up with Rhiannon who clearly seeks him out but avoids him day after day until he speaks to her. ' She had something to say to some persons here,' says Pwyll, ' if her *contrariness* allowed her to say it.' Here we have the supernatural powers of the Queen of *Annwfn*, a feature of the first element, reduced to the more lowly shyness of the Lady of the Lake and the teasing puckishness of the Pixies.

There are other traces both of the Lake legend and of the Pixie fairies in *Branwen*, but I make the suggestion here tentatively, because in order to establish their presence with certainty, it would be necessary to consider all the immense complex of contamination by contemporary folk tales which has made the *Branwen in Ireland* episode so puzzling. This portion of *Mabinogi Branwen*, which describes Branwen's degradation by being banished to the kitchen is, of course, a variant of *The Queen Falsely Accused*, the theme which was so popular in Europe in the middle ages and which is exemplified in the history of Constance in Chaucer's *Man of Law's Tale* and, of course, elsewhere in the *Mabinogion*, in the account of Rhiannon falsely accused and punished. It will be remembered that this was Branwen's punishment : ' They (the king's court) drove Branwen from the same chamber as the king, and compelled her to bake in the court, and bade the butcher, after he had been cutting flesh, to go to her and strike a blow on her every day.' Why the butcher ?

Now *Branwen* abounds in instances of one of the latest *cyfarwyddiaid*, through whose hands the story passed, forgetting to record the one fact that can make sense of the episode which they describe, and here is such an instance. It is consequent of his having previously omitted another detail necessary to make the story coherent, namely the false charge against Branwen for which she was thus punished. The charge was, I suggest, that she was one of the *Tylwyth Teg*—or whatever name the Welsh fées bore at that time. She was a foreigner, a native of the mysterious *Ynys y Cedyrn*, just as Rhiannon was a woman of *Annwfn*. Consequently she was to be *struck by the iron of the butcher's knife*, in order to drive her back to her own people, or at least to test her whether she was a fairy or not.

I said that the charge made against her personally is not specified. What is specified is that her husband's people in Ireland allowed a previous episode to rankle in their minds, when Branwen's brother Efnysyen, out of sheer love of mischief, had mutilated her husband's horses by cutting off their ears and tails, and ripping the flesh off their mouths. Now this irresponsible action, which has no motive in the Mabinogi as it stands, is precisely the kind of thing that the pixie portion of the fairy population are constantly doing, and proved beyond doubt to the people of Ireland that Branwen was a fée, because she was Efnysyen's sister, or as we would say in Wales today, was one of the *Tylwyth Teg*.

But that is not all, for the most important indication of the belief in Branwen's fairy connexion is contained in another part of the Mabinogi, where the action as described

is equally unmotivated.   After Branwen has been delivered
by her own people, the warriors of the Island of the Giants
(*Ynys y Cedyrn*), from her unmerited punishment, a peace
conference is held.   Everything goes well till suddenly the
puckish brother Efnysyen, seeing Gwern, Branwen's son,
going willingly to his other uncles says :

'Why does not my nephew come to me? Though he
were not king over Ireland yet would I gladly make
friends with the child.' ' Let him go to you and welcome '
said Bendigeidfran. The child went to him gladly. ' I
declare to God ' said he (Efnysyen) in his mind, ' that the
household little expects the slaughter that I am going to
cause now.' And he arose, and seized the child by his
feet and straightway before anyone in the house could lay
a hand on him, he plunged the child head first into the
blaze. And when Branwen saw her child burnt (*yn
boeth*) in the fire, she made to leap into the fire . . . but
Bendigeidfran held her.

Then there was general fighting in which all but seven
of the men of *Ynys y Cedyrn* and Branwen herself were
slain.

This was the ' slaughter ' which Efnysyen had in mind.

Of course, in this the final version of the *Mabinogi*,
Efnysyen's action explains why the two peoples, now at
peace, renew the fighting but, as I hope to prove elsewhere,
the story of Branwen, especially in this section, is hopelessly
tangled. In the original and well-authenticated form of
the tradition, the fighting took place in a raid on *Annwfn*
to capture the treasure of Pwyll, the Head of *Annwfn*, namely
the magic Cauldron of Resurrection, and no other motive
for the fighting was necessary. In any case, the result of an
action need not (as all mankind is tragically aware) be
consequent on the motive. It is probable that in an older
version it was Branwen herself who held the child in the
flames ; the curious detail of seizing him by the feet suggests
holding him *for a time* in the blaze rather than throwing him

into the fire, which could be much more effectively done by taking hold of him bodily.   As usual in the Mabinogion when two conflicting versions have to be harmonized, the *cyfarwydd*, knowing that tradition said that the act was Branwen's or even perhaps that Branwen had jumped with the child into the fire, covered himself against criticism by saying that Branwen *attempted* to leap into the blaze after him.

Now this episode is a confused version of the procedure for testing a Fairy Child or, in communities where the Fairies are definitely identified with Evil Spirits, a child of the Devil.   There were two main tests—you either threw the child into water, and if he swam, then he was a change-ling, a fairy child, or you held him in the fire and if he was burnt, then he was not a fairy ; if he did not burn then he certainly was a fairy.   Branwen had been charged with being a fairy, though the test of striking her with iron had apparently not been successful in driving her away, but the charge was still maintained and with special vigour against her son Gwern who was by this time in the royal succession.   In order finally to refute the charge, Branwen herself held Gwern in the flames, where everyone saw that he was *poeth*, ' burnt,' and so Branwen was vindicated. I suggest that the mysterious words which follow in the Mabinogi and which have puzzled all commentators, *Gwern gwngwch uiwch uordwyt tyllyon*, are a confused jumble of a sentence in the test or of a gloss which originally explained why Gwern was one of the *Morddwyd tyllion*, ' men with holes in their thighs.'   These holes were the result of his having been held in the fire.

7

While discussing the traces of the second and third elements in *Branwen*, I wish to remind you of another episode which, in itself a supremely interesting piece of folk-lore, may throw some light on the difficult question of folk-recollection in the traditions about an older race such as we saw inherent in the Lake legends. Into the already confused tangle of *Branwen* a long story has been inserted in the form of a conversation between Bendigeidfran and Matholwch, King of Ireland, explaining the circumstances in which Bendigeidfran obtained the miraculous *Pair Dadeni*, the ' Cauldron of Resurrection ' which he has just presented to Matholwch. According to my reconstruction of the probable growth of the *Branwen* complex, the original myth on which this episode is based was an account of an attack on *Annwfn* by the Hero, under whatever name he went, and the carrying away of *Preiddeu Annwfn*, ' the Spoils of Annwfn,' the King's Magic Cauldron, but this myth, originally the basis of the main element in *Branwen*, has in the final form of the Mabinogi been reduced to a mere shadow. It is probable that it had no previous connexion with the story of the Iron House to which it is here attached.

Bendigeidfran informed Matholwch that he had received the Cauldron from a man who, with his wife, had escaped ' from the iron house in Ireland when it was made red-hot over their heads.' Matholwch then took up the story and related how he was hunting on the top of a *gorsedd*, ' mound ' *near a lake*. He saw a large man of terribly hideous aspect with an even larger wife coming from the lake. ' In a fortnight and a month', says the stranger, 'this woman will give birth to a child fully armed.' Matholwch took them under his protection but within four months ' they made themselves hated and no one would countenance them, because they insulted and worried respectable men and women and were rapacious and truculent.' Matholwch could not get rid of them so he made an *iron* house for them. He plied them with food and drink and heaped charcoal all about the house. All the smiths in Ireland had been summoned, ' all the owners of tongs and hammer,' but *this was not to build the house*, since it was already erected. When they were drunk, they kindled the fire and worked the bellows, and so the heat of the iron house drove out the troublesome folk. By this time they had many descendants with them, but only two escaped, the husband and the wife. These two went to Bendigeidfran's realm where they greatly increased in numbers.

This episode is also found in an old Irish tale called *Mesca Ulad*, 'The Drunkenness of Ulster.' The victims in the Irish tale are Conchobar, King of Ulster, and his men, who are placed in the iron house by the King and Queen of Connacht. I hope to deal with the development of this story elsewhere ; let it suffice to say here, that in this instance at least, the Welsh version is more primitive than the Irish. The main points to be noticed are : 1. The strangers meet Matholwch on a *gorsedd*, a *sídhe*, invariably associated with visitants from another world. 2. The large man comes up from a lake. 3. He and his wife are clearly of a different race from the respectable Irish. 4. In the true pixie tradition, they cause mischief wherever they go. 5. There is no reason given in the Mabinogi why they should be placed in an *iron* house in order to burn them. The elaborate preparations of heaping charcoal up to the eaves of the house and summoning all the smiths in Ireland and having bellows to blow the fire would be unnecessary if they were simply locked up in an ordinary house built of wood like all the royal habitations of Ireland. Then the smiths of Ireland, ' all the owners of tongs and hammer ' are summoned *after* the iron house has been built! The essential feature is the iron, and the smiths were summoned not to build the house, but *because they wielded iron tools*, a detail carefully preserved in the narrative. This is well in the tradition of stories about the primitive inhabitants ; iron has a devastating effect on the fairy folk.

I suggest therefore that this episode in *Branwen* had originally nothing to do with the Cauldron of Resurrection but was attracted to it during the evolution of the Mabinogi, and that it contains a very specialised form of the Lady of the Lake type of story. This time the Lady is not a beautiful maiden but, like her husband, and as in many other accounts of the *Tylwyth Teg*, a hideous monstrosity. It may be suggested that we have here in this episode a confused mixture of the two most important fairy tests, Iron and Fire.

8

To return to our third element, the Pixies. They appear in *Lludd and Llefelys*, a complicated *märchen* which has been inserted in some of the Welsh versions of Geoffrey of Monmouth's *Historia Regum Britanniae*, but which is also preserved as a separate unit. In this story three ' plagues ' harass the Island of Britain ; we are not concerned with the second and third, but the first is described as follows : ' A race of men came called *Coraniaid*, and so great was their knowledge that there was not a word (*ymadrodd*) over the whole island however low it was spoken, if the wind met it, that they did not know. And for that reason they could not be harmed.' Lludd consulted his brother Llefelys, king of France, (the name *Llevelys* is clearly based on a scribal misreading of *Leueeis*, the Norman-French form of *Louis*), who made a long horn (of brass in one version) through which they spoke to one another, but their words were perverted and made to mean the opposite, so Llefelys perceived that the Devil was hampering them. He cured that trouble by pouring wine into the horn, and then gave his brother some *pryfed*, vermin, (or insects or even dragons) to be pounded in water and the mixture sprinkled on the *Coraniaid* and his own subjects in a joint conference of the two peoples. He thus destroyed the whole nation (*ciwdawd*) of the *Coraniaid* without harming his own.

This account seems to be a mixture of the second and third elements. The *Coraniaid* are a mischievous folk, possessing supernatural powers, but they are also a separate race living in the territory of normal men and interfering with their activities. In short, they are the same race as the unpleasant people who were exterminated in the iron house in Ireland. In two respects only does their history differ from theirs, they have supernatural powers and it is not said that iron is used against them, unless indeed the ' long horn ' was made of iron ; it is to be noticed that brass or bronze is not specified in some versions. Their ability to hear whatever the ' wind met,' that is whatever was in the air, is paralleled in many Welsh accounts of the Fairies,—that of Edmund Jones of Tranch, for instance, who says that ' the fairies knew whatever was spoken in the air without the houses, not so much what was spoken in the houses.' An early instance of this faculty is found in the Mabinogi of *Math fab Mathonwy*, where Math is described as knowing ' whatever whispering there be between men, however small it be, if the wind meets it.' That is to say, this attribute of the magician Math was derived from a ' pixie ' belief already existent.

An important feature of the *Coraniaid* legend is the fact that their name has survived into the first years of the nineteenth century to designate a savage and primitive race. In a hymn attributed to Anne Griffiths (1780-1805), but almost certainly by Edward Jones, Maes-y-plwm (1761-1836) are these lines :

> Caiff Hottentots, *Goraniaid* dua' eu lliw,
> Farbaraidd lu, eu dwyn i deulu Duw.

' Hottentots, *Coraniaid* of darkest hue, a savage host, shall be brought into God's family.'

9

We now come to the first element in my classification, the Welsh *Annwfn*, the other-world of gods and heroes, the most prominent and important feature in the Four Branches of the Mabinogi. How *Annwfn* itself was evolved in the imagination of our forefathers I have neither the occasion nor the ability to explain, but it will be necessary to give here some of the main facts about the inhabitants of this mysterious land and their interposition in the lives of ordinary men and women.

The *Annwfn* of the Mabinogion has two aspects, and it seems that the stories in the form in which we have them preserved in the complex of the Four Branches, are ultimately derived from two distinct sources. The first is mythological, in the strict sense of the word ; that is to say, the great figures of *Annwfn* were once definitely gods and goddesses with a mythology which can be easily reconstructed from their legendary history and from a comparison with classical and other mythologies. The second source is harder to define, and I hesitate to apply the name ' myth ' to the beliefs which are attached to it, and which are embodied in legends about the Happy Other-world, the Land of Youth, *Tír na nÓg*, the Land of Promise. There are two crucial questions —how did these two traditions of *Annwfn* come together, and in particular, had they come together in early times to form a unified mythology of *Annwfn* or were they only joined together when a belief in a world of féerie was evolved ?

The great figures of *Annwfn* appear in the *Mabinogion* in the second stage of their evolution ; that is to say, when they have ceased to be gods but have not yet become normally human ; whatever of their god-like attributes they retain are indistinct. They trail around them clouds of their old divinity, but they are clouds without much form or substance. In general it may be said that what distinguishes them from the ordinary human beings of Dyfed and Gwynedd (where most of the action takes place) is that they move and have their being in an atmosphere of *hud*, ' enchantment.' That enchantment is of two kinds ; it may be the possession of a mysterious power, as for instance, when Rhiannon's horse cannot be overtaken by the swiftest horse in Pwyll's stables though, to the onlooker, it only seems to move at a deliberate trot; or again it may be a malevolent magic which enables its possessor to shift his shape and to play tricks on his enemy. Gwydion, for example, can assume any form he wishes and enable others to do the same.   He can even make a woman out of flowers, and in the final scene of the Four Branches he encompasses the death of Pryderi ' by magic and enchantment.'

It will be necessary, at this point, to indicate very briefly what the plot or basic form of the Mabinogion was, as I have reconstructed it elsewhere.   The King of Dyfed was to marry a fairy visitant, Rhiannon, from the Other-world in circumstances somewhat similar to those of the country-man and the Lady of the Lake.   The fée had fled from her own country of *Annwfn* because she did not wish to marry a man of *Annwfn*, Gwawl fab Clud.   This started a feud between the Kingdom of *Annwfn* and the Kingdom of Dyfed. Gwawl turns up in disguise at the wedding and obtains possession of the bride, but Rhiannon had a superior magic and not only extricated herself from the result of the king's rash promise but subjects Gwawl to ridicule and insult. (*The first portion of the second part of* Pwyll).

The King of Dyfed and Rhiannon are married, but the Head of *Annwfn* still pursues his quest for Rhiannon.   By a trick of shape-shifting he assumes the form of the king and so is enabled to beget a child on Rhiannon who will be Pryderi, the Hero of the Four Branches.   (*First part of* Pwyll).

The feud between *Annwfn* and Dyfed continues.   When Rhiannon gives birth to Pryderi, the Head of *Annwfn* whom we may call Gwawl again intervenes.   He steals the child from Rhiannon's bed and substitutes a foal born on the same night.   The child is missing for a long time but he is at last recognised and restored to the queen.   (*Second portion of the second part of* Pwyll).   This concludes the original First Branch but whether the abduction of the child was, in the first form of the Mabinogion, identical with his abduction as a young Man in *Manawydan* it is difficult to decide.   If it was, then the original First Branch ended with the *Conception of Pryderi*.

Pryderi is now ruler over Dyfed, and the feud continues. Pryderi himself takes a hand in the struggle and he makes a raid upon *Annwfn* in a ship, since *Annwfn* is here conceived as being over the water.   As a result of the raid only seven of his men survive but they bring with them back to Dyfed the famous Cauldron of Resurrection which, by resurrecting the slain of *Annwfn* had enabled the Head of *Annwfn* to destroy the men of Dyfed.   (*Portions of* Branwen).   The feud continues, Pryderi is captured and carried away to *Annwfn*.   His mother and (originally) his father searched for him all over the land, and while he is away, a great desolation falls upon Dyfed ; it becomes the fabled Waste Land.   At last his mother Rhiannon descends into *Annwfn* and rescues him and when he is restored, fertility returns to Dyfed.   This is pure myth, in the strict sense of the term, and is, of course, found in almost exactly the same form in the Greek myth of Demeter and her daughter Persephone. Thus ends the Third Branch.   (Manawydan *and the second portion of the second part of* Pwyll).

The feud continues and *Annwfn* has the last word.   What the exact form was of the plot by which Gwawl enticed Pryderi to his death, it is difficult to know.   Whether Pryderi had stolen the Head of *Annwfn's* swine or his father had brought them up from *Annwfn* when he and the Head of *Annwfn* changed forms, I cannot decide, but the essence of the plot was that Gwawl gave Pryderi twelve horses with fine accoutrements, all created by magic, in exchange for the swine, and departed.   But the magic only lasted for a day, and Pryderi followed Gwawl to avenge the insult.   In the battle that followed, Gwawl by means of his magic obtained the victory, and slew Pryderi.   Thus the Saga of Pryderi, in four branches, came to an end.   (*Math fab Mathonwy*).

The above is the barest outline of what I maintain to be the original plot of the Four Branches.   A vast accumulation of the legends and folklore of Wales was squeezed—with consummate art it must be allowed—into this frame-work, so that we have the Mabinogion in their present astounding complexity.   All the legends and all the folklore do not belong to the same period of development—some, such as the Rape of Pryderi in *Manawydan* still retain an easily recognisable form of the basic myth which was aeons old when the Mabinogion were related by the *cyfarwydd*. Others again have lost their original form and most of their meaning, such as the legend of Rhiannon, ' the great queen ' who ruled over *Annwfn* with her husband Teyrnon, ' the great king.' Her myth during the passage of the centuries had become involved with that of the Great Mother, Modron, and her son Mabon, ' the great child,' and with another form of her own myth of *Epona* which, as Anwyl has suggested, represented her as a Horse-Goddess. Only confused traces of that myth are now found in the *Mabinogion*—her penance of acting as mare and carrying on her back the visitors to her husband's court, which pre-supposes a story in which she was accused of giving birth to the foal which her enemies had substituted for her child. Her legend became nonsense when, instead of this original accusation, the charge of having killed her child was substituted from the popular *Constance* legend.

Many other folk legends which had no part in the first form of the Four Branches are by this time inextricably mixed with the original theme. Some of them do not contain other-world features, as for instance, the *Eustace* legend of the long-suffering Christian Gentleman into the mould of which the Manawydan story is cast, and probably some of the onomastic stories, but others are accounts of magic and shape-shifting, as for instance the *Unfaithful Wife*, who in an earlier version of *Math*, transforms her husband into an animal. We have here a compound contamination, by which first the *Unfaithful Wife* has been intruded into the old Celtic legend of *Blodeuwedd and her lover* and then the resulting complex fitted into the myth of Lleu Llawgyffes, the god *Lugus* of the inscriptions.

Thus, in what I might call the *War-with-Annwfn* basis of the Four Branches, we have two main elements,—the legends of *Annwfn* themselves, some of which have been debased into mere stories about magic, and more recent folklore additions some of which also are concerned with magic. Whether all this latter element had originally a basis in myth, that is, in other-world belief we cannot at present discuss, but it is evident that here we have a considerable portion of the back-ground of the Fairy traditions of Wales. One question only is relevant and I am content for the time being to leave it as a question—had the belief in the Land of Faery, in other words belief about the *Tylwyth Teg* as such, had a period of independent life long enough to react on the final structure of the Four Branches? I can only say that I have been unable to discover even the faintest sign of the influence of faery, either as Welsh *Tylwyth Teg* or as the féerie of romance, on the Four Branches. Not only is the *Tylwyth Teg* not mentioned under any name, but there is no trace of that vast territory of magic over which Myrddin and his sister Gwenddydd preside and which is so prominent in French and Continental Romance. Which is only another way of saying that the Arthurian Legend with its Land of Féerie had not been evolved when the Mabinogion assumed their more or less final form in the tenth or eleventh century.

One detail, however, establishes a traditional connexion between the Fairies and the folk of *Annwfn*. When, in the Mabinogion, a man meets a stranger from *Annwfn*, he is seated on a *gorsedd*, a ' mound '; this corresponds to the *sídhe*, 'mound,' of the Irish tales, the home of the Fairy folk, which has come into English in the word *banshee*, from *bean sídhe*, ' a woman of the fairy mound.' Pwyll, when he meets Arawn, is on the *gorsedd* of Pen-llwyn upon Bwya, probably an old caer known today as Clegyrfwya ; he meets Rhiannon on the *gorsedd* of Arberth (Narberth). Matholwch is seated on a *gorsedd* when he sees the strange folk of the Cauldron come up from the lake, and I suspect that the *Llech* of Harlech, on which Brân is seated when he sees the ships coming from Ireland and where his followers feasted for seven years, was also a *gorsedd*.

10

We come finally to the one feature of Fairyland which has always intrigued the Welsh mind more than any other and which is known all over the western world ; it is the basis of Washington Irving's well-known story of *Rip van Winkle*. It is here that the old traditions of *Annwfn* intrude themselves most prominently into modern life, and when the *Tylwyth Teg* is mentioned in Wales it is to this particular story that one's mind naturally turns. Let me first of all give a résumé of this popular legend as it is related in every part of Wales though most of the records seem to have come from North Wales.

A young man was coming home late at night over an unfrequented country path. As he approached a secluded hollow in the moorland he heard music, the most enchanting he had ever heard. When he came to the hollow, he saw a company of the most beautiful women and men that eye had ever beheld dancing in the moonlight. As they whirled in a circle past him, he felt an overwhelming desire to join them ; the more he fought against it, the nearer to the dancers he was driven by some inward urge. At last, under the compelling charm of the music, his feet began to move to the rhythm of the dance and before he knew what he was doing he was among the dancers who gradually led him away into their abode. This was a magnificent palace full of such luxuries as he had never dreamt of, and on a board in the hall was a sumptuous feast to which he was invited. Dimly he remembered an old warning, that no one who ate of the fairies' food could find his way back to the upper world. However he feasted with his hosts and listened to their charming conversation and marvellous music, forgetting all his troubles and worries. He was told by his companions that he must on no account drink of the water of a magnificent fountain in the middle of the court-

yard. However, the temptation was too great ;   he
drank and immediately the palace and all its men and
women disappeared, and he found himself alone on the
bare moorland.   When he went home, he found that the
neighbourhood of his home was completely changed ;
no one in the village knew him, but an old woman had
heard her great-grand-father say that his great-grand-
father's brother had disappeared one night and had not
been heard of since.   He had been away for hundreds
of years.

Now compare that story with that portion of *Mabinogi
Branwen* which is called *Ysbyddawd Ben*.   Here is a résumé
of it :

' Cut off my head,' said Brân ' and bury it in London.
And ye shall be a long while on the way—in Harlech at a
banquet (*cinyaw*) seven years and the birds of Rhiannon
singing to you.   In Gwales in Pembroke ye will be four
score years.   And until ye open the door towards Aber-
henfelen in the direction of Cornwall ye may tarry there,
and the head be still with you uncorrupted.   And from
the time ye open that door, ye may not tarry there . . .'
And they went to Harlech, and began to sit and satisfy
themselves with food and drink.   And as soon as they
began to eat and drink, there came three birds and sang
to them a song and of all the songs they had heard, every
one was worthless (*difwyn*) compared with it.   The birds
were far out over the sea, but as easily seen as if they
were there with them.   The banquet lasted seven years.
From Harlech they went to Gwales.   There they had
a fair royal place above the sea, in a large hall with two
doors.   That night they feasted abundantly and merrily.
And for all the sorrow they had witnessed and that they
had suffered, no memory had they of that or of any woe in
the world.   They were there eighty years and they had
never known a merrier or more pleasant time.   They

had no more unease than when they first came there nor
did they find by looking at each other that they were any
older than when they came. They had no more unease
in the company of Brân's head than when he had been
there with them.

But one of them opened the door towards Cornwall and
at once they remembered all the losses they had ever had,
and all the kindred and companions they had lost as if
it had only then happened . . . And from that moment
they could not rest but started on their journey to London,
bearing Brân's head.

It is unnecessary to point out that in this passage we have
a slightly garbled description of the Happy Other-world
which is a feature of one kind of Irish story, notably the
Voyage of Brân. It is curious that, apart from a famous
passage in the *Book of Taliesin*, the ancient literature of
Wales has few reminiscences of this distinctive Celtic belief
of a land of music and joy and forgetfulness of all sorrow
which is variously called by the Irish the Land of Youth,
the Land of Promise, the Land of the Living, and the Island
of Women. It presupposes an aspect of *Annwfn* very
different from that kingdom of menace as we saw it portrayed
in the history of Pryderi, yet Rhiannon has her birds singing in this paradise and the description of the splendours of
Annwfn in the first portion of Pwyll is more applicable to
Annwfn as an Elysium than as the prison of *Mabinogi Manawydan*. It is probable that the *Annwfn* of the Mabinogion
is an incomplete conflation of the two aspects, but in the
folklore of the *Tylwyth Teg* the country of the Fairies is
pre-eminently a land of forgetfulness. The points in common
between the two summaries I have given above, the Rip
van Winkle type of legend and *Ysbyddawd Ben*, are : 1. It
is a land of music. 2. It is a land of feasting. 3. Time
does not exist there ; its inhabitants grow no older.
4. There is a definite taboo connected with life there,
something that, if done, will destroy the enchantment.

There has been much speculation on the anthropological significance of this Celtic Elysium, as any reader of Nutt's *Voyage of Brân*, for instance, knows.   I am not concerned with that side of the question, which is highly speculative. But no one, I think, will deny that at least half the lore of the *Tylwyth Teg* owes its origin to this ancient belief.